The Mighty Flame

Also by Greta Aurora:

The Dying Femme Fatale
Aphrodite's Daughter

The Mighty Flame

Greta Aurora

"It burns like blazing fire,
like a mighty flame.
Many waters cannot quench love;
rivers cannot sweep it away."

(Song of Songs)

Contents

Part 1 – A Drop of Sweetness

Part 2 – Lost in a Bitter Ocean

The Woman Who Loved Like No One Else

'Wake up, alluring soul!
Wake up, dejected mortal!
You have been sleeping too long.
Wake up, mysterious creature,
And let us hear your song!
Share with us the story of your misery;
Open for us the gates to your mystery!
Wake up, beautiful mortal!
You have been sleeping for centuries.
Awake, and let us step into your world –
Your world that had once collapsed
So tragically!
Let us see those golden ruins sparkle!
Let them bring back bright and dark memories!'

'Who's calling me after so many years of silence?
Who's woken me up from my peaceful rest?
Who are you and what do you want from me?
I'd suffered enough until my journey finally ended...
So why am I feeling alive once again?

I'd never ever asked for life, but I did ask for death.
And a sweet, gladsome death had saved me long ago…
So how dare you remind me of what I'd escaped from?'

'Please accept our apologies, gentle being
Of this hardened planet!
We have arrived here to find only faint memories
Of life left.
We found the cold skeleton
Of a civilisation
That had sunk from a warm ecstasy
Into a frozen damnation,
With a brief, sudden and loud explosion.
Through the surviving objects,
We've learnt about the emotions,
Which used to rule the beings
That used to rule this whole world.
Out of all these emotions,
We find most interesting the concept of love –
And we have chosen to resurrect you,
So you can explain its meaning to us.
For who would know love better
Than someone who was killed by it?
Lacking the perception of humans,

We need you to illustrate this feeling,
So we may get an insight into the life of your species,
And hopefully understand all that your kind had created:
Books, paintings, pieces of music –
All so beautiful and throbbing with energy;
All inspired by this strange idea
They had once called love,
And the resulting intimacy.
Do accept our apologies, once again,
For reminding you of your misery,
But you are the one who could help us understand
What constitutes this curious feeling.'

'So you want to know what love is?

I'll tell you all about it,

But beware:

Once you've heard my story,

You may want to leave this damned planet

As quickly as you can.

You are right; no one knows love better than me...

No one has looked it in the eye,

Begging for mercy,

For longer than I did,

Before my wish was finally granted.

Are you sure you want to know all about it?
Then listen carefully...
You know about human history,
So you must understand pain and suffering.
And if you've replayed the Final Blast,
You should know that its strength is paralleled
Only by the power of love in my heart.

I wasn't hit by a bullet;
I wasn't skinned alive;
I wasn't starved or beaten,
Yet I was begging to die.
I was subjected to the kind of torment
That takes away one's will to fight.
It's more excruciating than the ache of flesh and skin;
No physical pain can surpass the anguish of the heart.

To each person who's ever lived
Nothing could have been more tragic
Than their own personal tragedy.
I've never been a victim of natural disaster;
I've never had my home destroyed by a tsunami,
But my soul has its own earthquakes and wildfires.

What's worse than dying and wanting to live

Is living and wanting to die.

I opened myself up; my entire being...

I dropped my golden cloak so he could see

Everything, including my scars.

And in return, he deepened the cuts,

And filled me up with a dark,

Obscure pain

In the place of all the love

I'd given away,

Emptying my chest

Until but a cold, dried up cavity was left.

He never attempted to hurt me in any way,

Not physically or otherwise.

So you might ask why I was in so much pain...

Well, silence can hurt more than the cut of a sharp knife.

When you truly love someone,

You're ready to give your life,

Just to see them smile;

You'd set yourself on fire,

Just to warm them up

On a cold night.

Can you perhaps imagine what it feels like

When you'd die for someone
And they won't even give you
A small piece of their time,
A few fleeting moments of their entire life?
They won't move a finger for you,
When you're ready to jump out of the sky,
Just to have them glance at you
From the corner of their eye...'

'Thank you for shedding some light
On the painful mystery of love!
Thank you, crestfallen mortal!
But we are a little confused...
According to what we have learnt,
Love had been at least as beautiful
For many others
As unbearable it had been for you.
Therefore, we ask you,
Unfortunate soul:
Could those merry stories also be true?'

'Yes, you may have heard about the pleasure
Associated with love.
When two souls are on fire for one another,

They seek the illusion of becoming one...

This illusion is convincing when two bodies merge,

Making it the most magical of physical sensations.

But I'm not the best person, I'm afraid,

To describe the beauty of love...

My true speciality is pain,

For he, whose name I refuse to pronounce,

Rarely shared space and time with me.

On the few occasions,

When I was allowed to worship his skin,

I was only good enough to warm him up briefly.

He took me to Heaven with such little effort –

Perhaps with no effort whatsoever.

All he had to do was lie still

And let me cover him in my kisses...

That was the sweetest ecstasy,

The purest ocean of bliss...

And in that same ocean I drowned;

The bliss filled up my lungs,

As my heart was overwhelmed with euphoria,

And the rapture evaporated every drop of my blood.

I was killed by love...

Yes, he'd taken me to Heaven,

And we danced on the clouds...

But he then suddenly let go of my hand,
And I fell out of the sky alone...
The higher you go, the deadlier the fall.

This was my experience of love.
Have I helped you understand it by now?
Or shall I keep torturing myself,
Remembering everything I'd died to forget?

No answer... Are you still here?
Or am I talking to myself?
Well, it doesn't matter, really,
For the vortex of my memories
Has sucked me in so deeply,
I think I'm hopelessly trapped;
I'm so deeply trapped in this vortex
As my thoughts of him are trapped in my heart,
Eating it up to get to my chest,
Like they did then,
Before suffocating me in the end.

The power of true love laughs
At the power of the Final Blast,
Which destroyed billions of souls –

For love had destroyed many more,

All through the millennia.

Love is the kind of force

That could dissolve one's flesh and bones

So very easily.

As fire melts ice...

So the evil love looks for other challenges,

And instead it slowly dissolves

Something that has no physical form:

It aims for one's mind and soul.

And when love breaks you,

It hurts more than breaking all your bones.

Love threatens to kill you every hour

You don't spend with the object of your desire.

But it's the same force that keeps you alive

And keeps your mind set on the next time

You might be given the next dose

Of this cunning drug.

It keeps you alive so you can suffer more,

Only existing,

But never truly living.

Love creates a constant longing

To taste past flavours

And feel old and new sensations.
It's a ghostly mental prison –
A dark cell with a tiny window
To the grey sunset of the outside world,
With colourful photographs on the walls.
And it's guarded by the strong conviction
That the person in the photos is like no other.

Is there anybody out there?

Did I scare you away with my story of love and death?'

We are still here, alluring, dejected mortal.
It's just very difficult to find any words
Worthy of commenting on your heartfelt answer.
We can't even say how thankful we are
For the depth of your insight.
We just have one final question
Before we let you sink back into your rest.
As a reward for your much needed help
And an expression of our sympathy,
Would you like us to resurrect the man
Who'd ignited this love in your heart,
So you can see and feel him again,

One final time?'

'It's obvious what my mind would advise,
But you are speaking to my heart now.
I'm shaking with fright inside and out,
And only his touch could calm me down...
How could I say no to such an offer?
I'd die a million times to see him live for one second.'

The moment the woman was reunited
With the man for whom she'd lived and died,
She wrapped her arms around him tightly,
Knowing she wouldn't release him this time.
The air was set on fire between their eyes...
The man whispered, as he gently caressed her face:
'I love you... I'm just afraid...'
The fire in the air fuelled the blaze in their heart,
Making it too powerful for their souls to contain,
And for the first time, they truly became one:
They melted softly into one another,
And then perished in the fire of love.

All that had still been left of the human world
Was destroyed by the most powerful explosion
That has ever shaken this cold Universe.

Part 1

A Drop of Sweetness

The Common Thread

Love is the thread that connects us,

Flowing through all human blood,

Through all the generations,

Through past and present tribes and nations.

The cavewomen of the Stone Age

Felt their hearts race the same way

In response to a caveman's loving touch

Just as I do when I'm next to you...

Love has always been with us,

Like the soothing smile of the Moon.

Our Earthly Creation

I want to get to know every inch of your body;
I want to explore every bit of your skin.
I want to use
All of my senses
To get to know you,
Like no one has known you previously.
I want no secrets left;
I want to acquaint myself
With both your soul and your flesh –
All that which makes you yourself.

I could spend hours surveying
Every detail of your body;
Every birthmark, every wrinkle -
They're all like works of art to me.

Your sighs of pleasure are more beautiful
Than the most fabulous piece of music,
And time freezes when I listen to you...
It's the closest I can get to religious ecstasy.
And even Heaven must be a lie,

For there can be no greater bliss
Than what I feel when I'm by your side.
Every time my soul is burnt by your touch,
Angels are falling out of the sky.
They will never know our secret,
And neither will Satan or God –
Looking at us, they are clueless...
This euphoria wasn't created by either of them;
It's created and felt only by imperfect humans.

I Want Your Pain

I want to hold your hand,
Just so I can take your pain away.

I wouldn't hesitate for a moment
If I had the choice to suffer in your place.

I have felt so much pain already,
If I could, I'd make sure you don't feel any.

A little more torture would make no difference to me,
But I hate to think you are in agony.

I have captured the flames of Hell to keep you safe and warm,
And all I ask for in return is your shoulder to fall asleep on.

Yes, there's a fire burning in my eyes because I have seen
Hell;
I have tamed the flames and brought them back.

The worst is over; I have defeated Satan.
My eyes turn to Heaven... God's next...

Some days I hurt everywhere;
Other days I'm too numb to move.

Some days I want the world to end;
Other days I'm willing to pull through.

When I'm feeling down
And close to giving up,
I imagine holding your strong hand,
And it makes me want to survive,
Thinking of all the magical moments
Of our shared past and future nights.

Roses

I have blood red roses in my hands,

Grey earth crying chillingly under my feet,

Black clouds laughing with derision above my head,

A white room smelling of daisies behind me,

In front of me a rusty cross misspelling my name,

Around me emptiness gathering to take human form;

The abyss looks at me through love's soothing gaze,

When fate loosens its grasp on my hands and my soul.

Homesickness

I'm feeling homesick,
But don't know where home is.

I'm dying to go home...
But I'm feeling desperately lost.

I've looked North, South, East and West,
But I just don't know which way to head.

Perhaps my home is not a country or a house;
Perhaps my only home is in your arms.

Perhaps you'll allow me to feel at home by your side;
Perhaps love is home and home is love.

Angel

When I used to hear the word "angel",
I'd picture young, golden-haired girls
With feathery wings and bright halos,
But when I met you, that image was shattered.
Now I think of you every time someone mentions angels.

You don't have wings,
And I've never seen you fly,
Yet I could admire your angelic presence
All through the night,
In an attempt to discern your secret.
If I looked long enough,
I might be able to see your halo
In the dark.

You must be an angel;
No other creature
Could have this kind of power
Over my entire being,
And play these rusty strings
Inside my heart

So beautifully,

With the cleanest sound.

Under years of dust,

You've helped me find

My very own melody,

Which I sing with the kind of passion

I'd never known I was capable of feeling.

When you play this harp,

Which is yours primarily,

And less importantly my heart,

Your skills are otherworldly;

Your voice when you sing so heavenly,

The depth of your eyes so enchanting –

Just one glance,

And I feel like I'm dancing on a cloud,

In a divine trance,

Far above the crowd...

And when you stop,

I feel like falling from the sky,

And Heaven is no more...

But I know your wings will protect me

From the fall,

And you will guide me,

So I can dream on.

Just tell me you're an angel already!

Otherwise none of this makes any sense.

How else could you have beguiled me like this?

How else could you reach inside my chest

And take hold of my heart,

With your bare hands,

The way you have done?

You are my angel,

Even if you'll never reveal your true nature.

You mean more to me than you could decipher...

But I don't want to overwhelm you with my earthly desire.

You are the holy light at the end of the dark tunnel.

I'm only human: mortal and imperfect...

But you are an angel –

You must have many others like me under your spell.

Sweet Melancholy, Blissful Solitude

Sweet melancholy

Blissful solitude

Cold eternity

Dark moments without you

Beautiful pain

Soothing numbness

Homebound escape

Bursting nothingness

Wiged Man

I miss the inflaming warmth of your skin,

The beautiful tenderness of your lips,

The soft embrace of your body...

I miss the infinite depth of your eyes,

And I miss the stunning yet sad magic

Of seeing you spread your wings to fly.

Out of all the men who have crossed my path,

I've happened to fall for the freest one.

Loving a winged man is beautifully tragic...

No weights hold him back; he flies as he pleases.

He flies away from everyday life on golden wings,

And when he flies, his wings glimmer and mesmerise,

And they blind the women of the Earth...

The winged man forgets, but the women remember.

When he takes me with him above the clouds,

The world around us is melted by the heat of the Sun.

But then he gently places me back on Earth,

And I watch him fly gracefully further and further.

He's uncageable and so far away from me –

All I have left to lift me up is his winged memory.

Dark Dress

I wear this darkness
To hide some old scars.
If I let the mystery go,
How deep will you cut?

It's taken so long
To build this wall around me;
If you tear it down brick by brick,
My clothes might follow.
But will you protect me
From the cold?

The wall casts its dark shadow
Around me,
And the Sun may dazzle
My untrained eyes.
Will you cover my pale body
With yours
To guard it
From the strong light?

I'm too used to the dark...

And you seem to be the only spark

My eyes can bear.

I may throw away this dark dress,

After a long time, after all,

And I might learn

To find pleasure in warmth.

I've just grown too accustomed to the cold.

The only walls I still want

Around me

Are your arms.

I'm so complete,

And so perfectly,

Purely alive,

And I feel so very safe

In your embrace.

And your voice is the only guard

I can tolerate.

Will you still sing me a lullaby

After singing to thousands all night?

Love on the Horizon

In your kiss I feel the same gentle passion,
With which the sky desires the ocean,
And in your embrace I find the force,
With which the waves touch the shore.

The sea hurls itself at the land
With a life-transcending vigour and strength,
Before it softly withdraws, quietly, weakened,
Disappearing to recover in the distance.

I have no way of knowing when you'll appear next.
Are you the kind of wave that can be trapped
In a smooth and quiet bay, with me and no one else?
Or are you the kind that needs to leave and come back?

Would you ever give up your wave-form,
And find bliss in staying by the shore?
Or do you desire distance and freedom?
Does the sky remain faithful to the horizon?

Beatrice

Dante had seen his Beatrice

Only twice

In his entire life.

The first time he fell in love;

The second time he sunk

So deep,

There was no way out.

It seems

You're my Beatrice.

I've seen you more times

Than Dante had seen her,

And I even got a little taste of your love

And a lifetime's worth of inspiration.

So I haven't got anything to be ashamed of,

Have I?

Your being has become part of my soul –

I'll carry you in my heart and my words

For the rest of my life.

You'll be there, one way or another

In every sentence I'll ever write.

Black and Red

Black and red are my favourite colours –
Black, because I mourn every hour
Not spent naked in your arms;
Red, because it's the most passionate colour.

There's so much passion for you in my heart
That it can't all just stay inside;
A few drops have to escape,
Just so I don't drown.
The runaway drops mix with the black pain
And splatter onto the blank canvas of my life,
On which I write with my own blood.
My words bleed the most passionate love.

These Moments Are My Life

How much longer do I have to keep waiting?

How much longer does my heart have to keep racing,

Rushing and rushing to get to you?

May I be either loved or released soon?

When will I get to kiss you everywhere I can reach?

When will your intentions finally become clear?

Will you ever have mercy on me

Or is it my destiny to keep waiting eternally?

The moments I tend to pass

Chasing Future's smile,

Embraced by Past's strangling arms –

These moments are my life.

But without your breath on my skin,

I struggle to find a reason to live,

And without seeing life's smile in your eyes,

I can't seem to feel truly alive.

A Black and White World

It is a gift so precious

And a curse so vicious

To be able see colours

In a black and white world

Excuse Me, Sir

Excuse me, Sir... Do you remember me?
Excuse me, Sir... Do you recall those evenings?
Do you remember holding my hand so tenderly?
Did thousands of words carry no meaning?

Excuse me, Sir... Do you remember me?
Excuse me, Sir... Do you recall those nights?
Do you perhaps remember feeling my lips on your skin?
Do you recall how you quivered with delight?

Excuse me, Sir... I'm sorry about this long, awkward stare...
Excuse me, Sir... Could I be more than a happy coincidence?
Excuse me, Sir... Just a quick yes or no will do...
Excuse me, Sir... I'm in love with you...

My Only Dream

I don't dream of flowers;

I don't dream of gold and diamonds;

I don't dream of sparkling gifts;

I don't dream of anything

But the soft touch of your skin,

Which is more special and precious

Than all the fortune in the world.

When your naked skin touches mine,

I feel it somewhere deep, beyond my nerves;

I feel your nearness right in my heart...

I dream only of this breathtaking sensation;

It's rarer and much more real than genuine pearls.

The Wrong Man

I don't want what's best for me.

I don't want a dull, sane sobriety;

I want the thrill of madness.

I don't want to live in a safe captivity;

I want dangerous freedom instead.

I don't want to make the right decision;

I just want to fly freely towards danger.

I want to walk down the wrong street;

I want to kiss the man I shouldn't be kissing.

And if by accident, I do the right thing,

I won't refuse being rewarded.

But the only reward I want is him, the wrong man...

I don't seem to be able to love anyone else.

My Childhood Room

I want you to see my childhood room

While you're hearing my bones

Breaking into pieces

I want you to see the bed

On which I dreamt

Innocent dreams

I want you to see the heavy desk

At which I wrote down

Heavy thoughts for the first time

I want you to see my childhood room

I want you

I want you

I want you

I want you to see my childhood room

While you're hearing my heart

Breaking into pieces

I want you to see my childhood room

I want you

I want you

I want you

I want you to see my childhood room

I want you to see that picture of Marilyn Monroe

On my wall

And my dead mother's painting

Of a couple dancing

I want you to see the things

That make me

And break me

I want you to see my childhood room

I want you

I want you

I want you

I want you to see my childhood room

I want you to see my hometown

I want to show you

The streets where I walked for the first time

And I want you to see the sharp edges

Of this town

Where I tripped and fell and hurt my knees

For the first time

Long before I first fell into your arms

Or rather jumped

Propelled by that first bruise

And others I've gained over the years

On my knees

And other parts of my body

And the scars

I tend to forget about

When I'm close to your heart

And the wounds

That happened once I left my childhood

And that room

I want you

I want you

I want you

I want to see all of you

And I want you to see

All of me

I want you to see my childhood room

I want you

I want you

I want you

I want all of you

And I want you to want all of me

The Final Phase

I want to flee

From this damned moment

In human history

Where the physical rules

And you can invite the whole world

Into your bedroom

And no one blinks an eye

But if you talk about love

Everyone laughs

I have more than I would have had

In any other century

But what good is that

If I am forced to feel less?

Yes, we have a lot

Yet we always want more

Impossible to satisfy

I see flashbacks of the orgies of late Rome

The First Time

Looking back, my story hadn't fully begun
Until you kissed life into me;
Until the moment you touched my heart
And held onto it...
Or, rather, it got stuck in your hand,
And now you don't know what to do with it.
I'll never forget the moment our lips first met,
And I'll recall it every hour until they meet again.

You cannot possibly understand
How much that first time had meant...
And every time after that
I fell deeper and deeper into your sweet trap.

The first time my naked skin touched yours
I felt like I'd arrived; I'd finally come home.
And when I'm not with you, I feel homeless...
I'm so happy just to exist in your beautiful presence.

The Universe and Your Kiss

The whole world lives in the warmth of your touch;
It comes to life the moment I feel your skin.
All of nature's beauty is hiding in your smile,
And the universe is made complete by your kiss.

When we're lost in a lazy, burning embrace,
There's nothing else I could possibly wish for.
I have all I need when I feel your fingers on my waist
And anywhere else they might choose to explore.

Your eyes are crystal clear ponds in a sunny oasis;
They mesmerise me and wash away the dull reality.
The heat of your glance burns my clothes until I'm naked
And ready to bathe you in bliss, wanting you to bathe in me.

I feel at home as parts of my flesh find their equivalent,
When our bodies press so firmly and tightly together,
It's impossible to tell where you begin and where I end –
And that moment love bursts out of the exploding desire.

The hurricane of passion mixes our body parts

Until we don't know what belongs to whom,

And it blends and melts our souls into one,

And I wouldn't want to survive if it wasn't for you.

Uncertain Times

Stillness

Ripple

Silence

Clamour

Two hands reaching

For one another

But only touching

In a dream

Moments

Short years

Frozen

Horizons

Time is precious

Like tiny diamonds

It slips between our fingers

Like sand and pearls

Kisses

Whispers

Lightening

Thunder

Two bodies merge

And then get torn out

Of one another

In these uncertain times

Your Body, Your Love

Looking at your face in the gentle light

Of the smiling stars

That witnessed our otherworldly love,

My mind drifts

And I doze off

Into a shallow sleep,

Like dipping my toes

Into the warm sea

And jumping back to the shore

Immediately,

Because every moment

Here with you in this bed

Is worth treasuring.

I want to be present

To hear your heart beat

And feel your breath

On my cheek,

Not to waste any of these seconds

For they're all lovelier than the most beautiful dream.

The Moon surrenders to the dawn

Like I surrendered to your kisses

A few hours ago –

Hands exploring,

Like a born wanderer first leaving home,

Primal instincts kicking in,

Before even stepping through the door.

The air steaming...

Two hearts on fire, boiling...

Your flavour mixing with mine on my lips,

Not knowing whose taste it is,

And it doesn't matter...

The whole world is pulsating

Like our bodies

Traveling through the universe,

Blessing...

Curse...

Blessing...

Curse,

Curse,

Curse...

You taste so incredibly sweet...

But even honey turns sour

When I remember you must leave.

And you also awake at the break of dawn...

With fresh memories of the night,

We both want more...

We see our reflections in each other's eyes.

You pull me closer to you under the sheets,

And here we are, sharing this dream,

Against all the odds...

To quench my morning thirst,

I want all your drops,

But let's feel one another's hills and mountains first...

Our sighs are the music to nature's art show...

And even the hot plains aim for Heaven.

Our bodies become one,

Like two small waves in the ocean

Uniting the moment they touch.

It's not enough

To feel your skin on mine...

I want it inside,

Filling me up to the brim,

Until I'm choking on it.

Once our flesh is throbbing as one

And our blood is hot as lava,

Ready to erupt,

There are no more frontiers left.

The dam explodes but the river survives...

There's no closer, and I feel content holding your hand.

Play Me

You create the most beautiful music
Within my soul
When you run your fingers all over my skin
For brief moments of a blissful eternity
It feels like swimming in the purest ocean
Of fluid passion
Your playing is proof that Heaven exists
We just have to create it ourselves on Earth

And you're playing me like an instrument
Making me produce sounds I didn't know I had
In me
So please play me

Play for me
Play anything you want
Play me
Play these strings
Only you can see
I want your music to fill up
My entire being

And I'll dance
I'll dance for you
Like I've never danced
For anyone else before

Play me
Pull my strings
To the rhythm of your music
To the rhythm of your heart
To your eye's delight
And I'll move
Any way you want me to
And I'll move only for you

Time Travel

Have you ever wondered who sang the first ever melody

And what it sounded like?

Or who composed the first piece of music

That brought tears to someone else's eyes?

Would you like to travel back in time with me

And find out?

Before they made music,

Humans must have learnt to love

And feel pain;

But to me, these two are the same.

Would you sit with me by the fire

On a pure, primeval night,

Looking up at the virgin, star-filled sky,

Holding my hands tight,

As if you never wanted to let them go,

Seeing an even brighter fire burning in my eyes?

Would you agree,

Having travelled back 30,000 years,

30 wouldn't seem so many?

And it wouldn't matter where we'd both started our journeys

In a world before time and before countries.

Would you sing me a lullaby

While I'm listening to your heart

Beautifully beat,

As I gently weep

Ecstatic tears?

I tend to struggle to fall asleep

When reality feels like a dream.

But I wouldn't even mind

Spending one long, sleepless night

Laying by your side,

Looking at your face in the gentle moonlight,

Like I've already done once before,

When an otherworldly feeling took control

Of my soul –

I couldn't take my eyes off you,

And even after you'd left in the morning,

Your image had stuck in my head,

And from that point

There's been no turning back.

Your smell has faded from my skin

And your taste from my lips,

But this feeling you've given me

Is still lingering.

And since that moment,

I haven't desired anyone else.

I've tried looking into other eyes but I missed your lips,

And the more someone else has tried to impress me,

The more clearly I remembered all of your kisses.

There's not much I wouldn't give

To lay my head on your shoulder,

And feel your hands on my body,

Wherever they choose to travel.

I guess you just wanted to laugh

And touch and perhaps feel a little bit –

And all that should've been enough

Also for me...

But I got lost swimming in the warm pond of your eyes,

And I'm afraid of drowning,

Because I still haven't found the way out.

How embarrassingly pathetic of me...

I'm sorry to make something light-hearted and sweet

Into something heavy, bitter and deep.

Would you follow me to ancient Egypt, Greece and Rome?

We could listen to mystical chants and haunting choral songs.

And while our ancestors worship their imaginary friends,

I'd perform my own ritual for you on a deserted island.

We could bathe in the pristine Nile and the Mediterranean,

And I'd want every drop of you I can have.

But I'd also love to hang out with some goddesses;

I have a lot to learn about confidence and dignity.

Next, can I interest you in the Enlightenment?

Everything will accelerate once we're there...

And I'll start feeling like I'm running out of time –

How many more centuries do I need to pour my heart out?

And how many languages do I need to learn to speak,

Before I find the words to express how you make me feel?

I'd watch you exchange ideas with Mozart, Beethoven, Liszt,

And I'd know I'd have to hurry up when we meet Debussy.

I might finally manage to speak my mind

By the time we step inside a smoke-filled blues bar.

Or perhaps it would be in the jazz era

That I'd manage to open up at last.

I just hope it wouldn't be in the Sixties,

Because then I wouldn't remember any of it.

And here we are in the 21st century,

When everybody is confused about everything,

But nobody is as confused as me.

Will I ever be good enough for somebody?

I have so many questions to ask,

And so much to say,

But I don't want you to laugh

At me and my naïveté.

Would you be amused

If you knew

How often I think about you,

And how many desperate attempts I've made

To be completely honest with you, yet I've always failed?

Would you care?

Would you even believe

I've never craved anyone else

Like this,

And there's no one I'd rather wake up next to?

Would you think I'm crazy

To fantasise about sharing my life with you?

Would you smile in disbelief

If I told you I saw something special in you

The very first time

I looked in your eyes?

And that vision has only become more powerful,

More intense

And more tragically beautiful

Every moment our hands met,

But it's never been clear,

And I haven't figured out what it means

Just yet.

It hasn't weakened its grip on me,

Although I've tried to fight it with all my strength,

I promise.

There was one time I'd thought I might have been winning;

A few days, perhaps weeks,

When I seemed to have convinced myself

I was strong and complete.

I'd resolved to travel far away from your spell,

But you were travelling on the same train...

And that was the surreal sabotage of my planned escape.

Every single night

Since I last kissed you goodbye,

I've imagined you were in my bed

After I switched off the lights,

And I've played entire conversations in my head.

But when you were right there in the crowd,

Within easy reach of my shaking arms,

My sight became a wet blur,

And I wouldn't have been able to say a single word.

But if I'd been less of a coward,

It would have gone something like this:

'Excuse me, Sir... Do you remember me?
Excuse me, Sir... Do you recall those evenings?
Do you remember holding my hand so tenderly?
Did thousands of words carry no meaning?

Excuse me, Sir... Do you remember me?
Excuse me, Sir... Do you recall those nights?
Do you perhaps remember feeling my lips on your skin?
Do you recall how you quivered with delight?

Excuse me, Sir... I'm sorry about this long, awkward stare...
Excuse me, Sir... Could I be more than a happy coincidence?
Excuse me, Sir... Just a quick yes or no will do...
Excuse me, Sir... I'm in love with you...'

After I got home,
The painful longing filled up my heart
And overflowed.
If I hadn't cried, I would've laughed
At my own pitiful remnants of hope.
I closed my eyes and curled up,
Like a cold and unwanted baby,
Trying hard to feel your arms around me.

Then my tears ran out and I smiled,

Imagining how content you were with your life –

You have the power to make thousands happy

All at once,

So why would you even care about someone like me

Who's just a face in the crowd?

All I can hope to do is use your happiness as inspiration

To create my own joy and unwavering satisfaction.

We've been to the past –

Would I be too greedy

If I asked

If you wanted to travel to the future with me?

To tell the truth,

I know I shouldn't hope for time travel of any kind

With you.

Some people were just born to dream

But never to get what they seek.

Some of us are destined to love

Hopelessly

And disturbingly deeply,

But not to be loved,

So all we can do is find beauty

In our lonely melancholy –

And this beauty is what makes us write

Long, silly poems like this,

And compose gorgeous tunes

For happy couples to cuddle to.

You have no idea how I wish

I could run my fingers through your hair

And taste your lips

Just once again.

But no amount of wishing

Is going to change anything.

But there's one thing I can perhaps ask for...

Could you use a heavy and blunt hammer made of sincerity

And shatter my hopes

With the force

Of all the advantages you have over me

(Including experience and felicity)?

And from the splinters of my hopes

More poetry and music shall be born –

But I'll keep the inspiration a secret.

I've tried destroying this suffocating hope,

But don't seem to have the strength

To do it on my own,

Even though I detest asking for help.

Sometimes a bit of cruelty is a prerequisite for kindness.
And the more direct you can make the blow of the hammer,
The sooner I can get back to writing about femmes fatales,
And the sooner I can try to look elsewhere for passion.
Please, please break this cage and free me from your spell,
So I can be stronger by the time we might meet by accident.

But a little bit of spark will remain for sure,
Even after the hope finally dies,
And I'm so glad to know I can always see you –
I just have to close my eyes.

When We Meet Again

What will his kiss feel like

When our lips reunite

After such a long time apart?

Will I be able to taste the thoughts

That warmed him up

On nights he felt cold?

Will his tongue tell me stories

That no voice could speak or sing?

Will his hands explore forgotten lakes and hills

Only to realise they've arrived home finally?

When we meet again, will he stay?

Will he recognise and appreciate

The value of the landscape we share?

Or will he leave again?

A Drop of Sweetness Lost in a Bitter Ocean

You are a drop of sweetness lost in a bitter ocean.

Your golden glow captures my attention,

And the freeness of your fall hypnotises my eyes.

You are a drop that sparkles in the sunlight,

And then disappears in the water,

Never to be found;

A dissolving genuine pearl,

A rare diamond that will never be mine.

You are a drop of sweetness lost in a bitter ocean.

You are on my mind whenever life feels unbearable.

You are hard to let go of, but you drip off me,

Rushing to the ocean on the wings of a beautiful melody,

Escaping between my fingers.

I admire your journey,

Yet a fall is a fall, no matter how glamourous...

But my silver glow will persist when you reach the ocean.

Part 2

Lost in a Bitter Ocean

The Mighty Flame

You ignited the primeval fire in me;

Solomon's mighty flame.

And you left it to be extinguished,

Carelessly walking away,

Never looking back.

But it has been burning ever since then —

It has never weakened,

Not for a single moment.

Fed by nothing

But my gilded thoughts of you,

It has been glowing and growing

Into something almost implausibly forceful.

It has grown into

An intoxicating blaze

That is now stronger than I am.

Its fumes have dressed my mind in a haze,

And now I'm trapped in this maze...

This fire is unquenchable.

There is not enough water in the world

To wash it away...

Do I have to drown myself to escape?

Is that the only way?

The mighty flame

Shines its light on my gilded thoughts,

As though there was a halo

Or the King's crown

On your head.

I have been mesmerised

And hypnotised

Into believing

You could never do me any harm.

It is unthinkable

That you would ever use your power

To burn

And hurt,

When you could use it to elevate

On the warm wings

Of the blaze.

Yes, you have the power to lift me up –

How could you possibly use it

To bring me down?

You could raise me

Towards the Sun,

Which could be the final stop –

My ultimate home,

Once I have let go

Of all hope

And chosen to depart...

Once the fire has torn my heart apart.

But you would never choose to elevate me.

And you would never climb a palm tree

To get to me,

Like Solomon did

To get to a rose of Sharon –

A lily of the valleys,

A lily among thorns.

Am I perhaps a thorn?

Am I too appalling

To even behold,

Let alone interact with?

Is that why you have turned your back

On me?

Or is it because you think

There are 700 women waiting?

But you are not Solomon,

And I know

I am not a thorn.

I am just me,

But I would climb and crawl

Any distance to you

On my hands and feet,

But you don't want any of my fruits.

I know you can't feel the same warmth

I am feeling,

And perhaps never have before

And never will...

But can you not feel anything at all?

Is it only my privilege,

Or rather, damned, tragic ability,

To feel with this blazing intensity?

Echo

On my evening stroll,

In search of tranquillity,

Yearning to soothe my soul,

I came upon a pristine spring,

Away from all the noise,

Far away from the city.

No one had heard my voice

For a long-long time...

I'd decided not to say a word,

For I'd once used language so cunningly,

My speech got me into terrible trouble.

I was punished by being deprived

Of my ability to express my thoughts,

But the evil woman let me keep my voice...

And, since then,

I have only been able to echo

What others have said.

I'd rather be deaf or mute...

But I wasn't allowed to choose.

On my peaceful evening stroll,

I came across a man named Narcissus...

Narcissus...

Narcissus...

Narcissus...

Narcissus...

He didn't see me at first,

But I couldn't take my eyes off him...

I had no means of catching his attention,

But every piece of me yearned for his kisses...

Kisses...

Kisses...

Kisses...

Kisses...

A human statue sculpted to perfection,

With a captivating aura and energy

Matched by no other...

No other...

No other...

No other...

No other...

My soul was flooded

With the most intense passion...

Passion...

Passion...

Passion...

Passion...

And I couldn't help but follow him

Into the dark forest of grim trees –

A forest of childish confusion

And bitter tears...

Tears...

Tears...

Tears...

Tears...

For I was not capable

Of giving a voice

To my thoughts of admiration.

I couldn't even say hello,

Just to see that divine countenance

Acknowledge my earthly presence.

I could not have been so bold

As to reach for that precious hand,

Which, I felt, could play sacred chords

That would resonate deep within my soul.

But I'd have certainly let him hold my hand,

Had he ever wished to do so.

My steps on dry leaves

Did not remain unheard for long.

Being unable to speak...

Speak...

Speak...

Speak...

Speak...

Any words of true meaning...

Meaning...

Meaning...

Meaning...

Meaning...

Shall I still reveal myself?

Is there a chance he'll understand me

And feel the same way?

I did not dare...

Dare...

Dare...

Dare...

Dare...

But then he turned around and said:

'Who's there?'

I repeated helplessly, on edge:

'Who's there?'

There...

There...

There...

There...

He then caught sight of me...

Our eyes met...

I could not resist,

And attempted to throw myself

In his arms,

Propelled by fiery desire...

Desire...

Desire...

Desire...

Desire...

But he escaped from my embrace...

And he knelt by the spring

To admire himself instead,

Just like I'd been doing...

I knew my disability would lead me

To the grave...

Grave...

Grave...

Grave...

Grave...

Cursed into this endless, silent night

I could not stay.

I was eaten by my own fire,

And only my echo remained...

Remained...

Remained...

Remained...

Remained...

Amber

Let me tell you a story about a girl!

Her name was Amber.

She passed away tragically young.

She wasn't murdered,

She wasn't the victim of any crime,

She didn't harm herself,

And she never had an accident.

She wasn't even sick –

She was perfectly healthy,

According to all quantifiable measures,

The doctors she'd visited told her.

Her blood tests showed no problems at all,

And the PET scan didn't reveal any faults.

Heart, lungs, stomach, liver and kidneys

Had all been working normally.

Yet, Amber felt an ever-increasing pain,

Which no one could explain.

The pain had started in her chest

At an unidentifiable point,

And then it started to spread,

Intensifying progressively.

It spread into her heart first,

And then it filled up her lungs.

Then it conquered her stomach and liver,

Before slowly crawling up her spine,

Until it arrived in her brain...

There was no cure, no explanation,

No hope, no escape.

The doctors were trying to figure out

What was wrong with her organs,

Never taking into account

Those way deeper realms,

Which are hidden even from the MRI machine.

No doctor had ever asked how she was feeling

Beyond her tissues, flesh and skin,

And no one had realised

That her physical pain was nothing

Compared to her suffering deep, deep inside.

'Have mercy on me!' She cried,

And her wish was granted, eventually.

When she finally died,

With an ecstatic sigh of relief,

A photograph fell out of her hand:

A photograph of a man

Who'd never know

About the pain he'd caused.

Amber was lonely but in love;

What a strange combination...

The love first ate her heart,

And then it destroyed the rest of her

Until nothing was left of the girl.

Let Me Burn in Your Fire

When you love someone with so much passion
As a planet loves its only star,
It seems almost unthinkable
That they'd have no place for you in their heart.

I'm yearning to be closer to your fire –
The only light on my empty sky –,
But there's a constant distance between you and I,
As I fly through life
Never touching anyone,
Only dreaming of your fire,
Even though I'd get burnt badly, I know,
If I got too close...
But that thought makes me want you even more.

Let me burn in your fire...
Let me burn in your fire...
Burn me until my heart dries up...
Burn me until I breathe my last...
Let me burn in your fire...
Let me burn in your fire...

As I whisper your name with my last sigh...

Burn me until I forget how to love...

Let me burn in your fire...

Let me burn in your fire...

Burn me until there's nothing left of me...

What a beautiful way to die...

Being slowly consumed by your kiss,

In the boiling embrace

Of your flames,

Feeling no pain,

Only your warm gaze

On my dry skin...

When my eyes have burnt out,

Once I'm not able to see,

Your touch will be amplified...

I'd be content just to die

By your side.

I have no bold hopes

To be alive

And be yours.

All I want from life

Is to be eaten away by your fire...

But you want me neither dead

Nor alive...

Wet Eyes

In the morning, moments after waking

With wet eyes,

And just before surrendering

To that sweet unconsciousness

At night,

Thoughts of you occupy my mind,

Leaving no space for anything else -

Like dreams, they're colourful and vivid

Often more so than reality itself.

The pain doesn't stay in my eyes;

The wetness travels further and further down

Until I'm bathing in my tears,

And they fill me up deep inside...

I'd be ready if you wanted to bathe with me.

Loving in Sodom and Gomorrah

I told my therapist I was in love with a man

Whom I haven't seen for nearly a year,

And she said I needed something more potent

Than talking therapy.

Then I went to see a psychiatrist,

And now I'm about to take some sertraline –

Because being in love is a mental illness

In the 21st century.

People rarely talk about love

In this modern-day Sodom and Gomorrah.

No one writes love letters –

We feel lucky if we get a text back,

Or if they follow us on Twitter,

Or like all our posts on Instagram.

It can be intimidating, in the age of the physical,

When someone talks about emotions,

Longing to build a genuine connection.

How many times do I have to kiss you

Before it's appropriate to write a poem for you?

And how many more nights do we need to spend together

Before I can tell you: the poem has turned into a collection?

I should probably wait a lot longer...

But I revealed all of this to the psychiatrist.

He said, 'people don't talk about these things'.

And he increased my dose to reduce my risk of writing anything.

Shadow

I'm only a shadow of who I once was.
I'm the shadow you cast
Over the golden statue
Of the goddess of beauty and love.

I was once a statue myself,
But my porcelain skin has turned to glass.
No one will ever see me again;
I'll fade away, not being warmed by your touch.

Another man had reached for my hand once;
I reached back, but he couldn't see me anymore.
Without you, I can't step out of the dark...
But when you walk by, I'm just a shadow.

Marionette of the Universe

The English countryside embraced me,

Tightening its grasp,

Until I could hardly breathe.

The green fields were melted by the Sun

On one of the year's hottest days,

And, like a whirlpool of fluid metal,

The magnetic fields pushed me away,

And then dragged me back even closer.

I'm no more than a toy of nature;

The subject and object

Of its cruel sense of humour.

One moment I feel strong and invincible,

Close to the centre of the Universe;

The next moment I feel as though

I've fallen into a black hole,

From which there's no turning back.

That hot day, I got on a train

In an attempt to outrace nature,

Naturally bound to fail.

Then, it seemed, my prayers were answered:
There he was, right next to me –
The one man occupying my thoughts
And cunningly hijacking my dreams.
I'd prayed we could fight nature together,
Forming our very own team,
And I felt honoured to be allowed to share
One more piece of reality with him.
He'd already given me some moments
I knew I'd never be able to forget;
The happiest moments of my life...
I'd have never guessed he'd be able to top that.

The choking day gave way to a passionate night.
That night he fed me the world's sweetest nectar,
More intoxicating than the strongest wine...
And he enticed me into believing
He had some even sweeter drops for me,
I just had to wait one short week.
It was a night I'll remember on my death bed,
And I'll smile,
With tears of contentment in my eyes,
Recalling that time I felt truly alive.

After this ecstatically surreal experience,
I thought to myself the next day,
He'd surely be dying to see me again...
But, unlike me, he didn't want a team mate,
But a doll-like plaything
With a young fire that needs no rest,
And a youthful naivety to match.

Now, I'm willing to surrender to nature's will
Any damned moment of my worthless life...
But how could I have let myself be played with
By someone who also has a beating heart?
Although I'm not sure his heart works
The same way mine does,
And I don't even know he has one for certain.

I was born to be a helpless marionette
Of an invincible Universe...
And I have also somehow become
The puppet of a mere mortal.

I'm Sorry

I'm sorry I cried the last time I saw you,
And I'm sorry I had tears in my eyes the time before.
I'm sorry I find it hard to control myself,
Whenever you are within an arm's length.

I'm sorry I've allowed pain
To be the building blocks of distance,
And I'm sorry I can't escape
Far enough from your spell.

I'm sorry I couldn't hold it all in anymore;
I'm sorry I had to let those pathetic words out;
I'm sorry I can't let you go;
I'm sorry you're always on my mind.

I'm sorry I can't get you out of my head;
I'm sorry I love you like no one ever has,
And no one ever will.
I'm sorry.

You Deserve More

The cloud of bitter doubt over my head
Cries a corrosive desperation on me,
Burning my skin and eating into my flesh,
And replacing the blood in my arteries.

I choose to reach out to you once again;
I extend my trembling, weakening arms.
This time it could be much different;
This time we could perhaps talk about love.

Doubt turns into devastation when I don't hear from you,
(But I'd use my last drop of strength to keep reaching)
And I feel miserably guilty every time I do
Because you deserve someone much better than me.

You deserve the most beautiful woman
With the body and soul of a goddess;
You deserve the greatest, the nicest, the best...
I'd give you everything, but you deserve more than that.

My Creation

I love seeing you with no clothes on
And feeling your skin's beautiful warmth,
Yet I've dressed you up in my imagination.
I've dressed you in a fantasy of gold,
Studded with diamonds of bright colours.
In the end, I've created someone new,
And I've been admiring my creation...
But it's someone barely resembling you.

I've created a parallel Universe
Where you care about me and my words,
Both loudly spoken and shyly written.
But in this dark, stark reality,
You really don't care about me.
I'd give everything for a bit of your attention,
But to you, I'm little more than a stranger.

I can't stop worshipping the man I've created –
I'm mesmerised by the inebriating mystery
Of this gentle, sweet, kind-hearted entity.
The name might be all you share with him,

But my pagan soul needs an idol, it seems.
Does the man I love only exist in my dreams?

Is my vision of you my very own golden calf?
Are you really not the man that I love?

Who's this creature who's become
Such an important part of my life?
Is he not made of human flesh and blood?
Am I in love with an idea?
Is it a mere fantasy that keeps me awake at night?
Will I never know who you really are?

Your Eyes

Your eyes haunt me
Like a distant memory
Of happiness so uncanny
I don't think I deserved it

From that very first time
I got lost in your eyes
On a cold night
Looking for some warmth
I didn't know
I'd get trapped for so long
Losing any desire to be free
And I see you in every dream
And I'm losing interest in reality

I wanted you so deep inside me
Like I've never had anybody
And now your eyes won't leave
Even though your body is not here

When you left

You left me under your spell

And now your spell is all I have

And the memory of your eyes

Looking down

Wanting to penetrate into mine

Until we became one

And I opened up

So I could accept you completely

And now I'm lying here

Cold and empty

With the memory

Of your eyes

Keeping me

From sleeping at night

And also preventing me

From waking

So I merely exist

I don't live

And I exist only for you

But you don't seem to think

I can be of any use

My mother once told me...

My mother once told me, one day I'd be in love.
She said I'd just know it; I'd feel it in my heart.
It would beat a little faster and I'd feel out of breath,
Whenever I saw his face, she said.

My mother once told me, love was so beautiful –
She said, love gives you strength and invigorates you.
And she said, birds would sing whenever I'd think of him,
And the smell of roses would fill the air when we kissed.

But there's no birdsong, only screams of shattered dreams,
And my mother has been dead for many years.

She told me, love makes everything feel so light;
It makes you weightless, so you can walk on clouds,
And there would be rainbows in the sky
The moment it occupied my heart.

She said it was something to look forward to,

But not something to force; it just happens to you.

I've been looking forward to it and now it's happened to me,

But it feels very different to how my mother described it.

There are no rainbows, only cold, colourless tears,

And my mother has been dead for many years.

I Shouldn't Have to Fight So Hard
for Love

I shouldn't have to fight so hard for love
I shouldn't have to beg for my prison guard's attention
I shouldn't have to weep dreaming of your touch
I shouldn't have to believe I deserve no affection

I shouldn't have to fight so hard for love
I shouldn't have to see the indifference on your face
As you glance at my gift – a huge piece of my heart –
Only to irresponsibly throw it away
While you say thank you for every piece of rubbish
You're given by everybody but me

I shouldn't have to fight so hard for love
I shouldn't have to constantly question if I'm good enough
I shouldn't have to keep making sure you're alright
While you forget I'm also in pain sometimes

I shouldn't have to fight so hard
For your second-hand love

In Love with a Hitman

I love you more than I could love

Anyone else.

I want to feel that loaded gun

Again and again,

Even though I know

One day I'll be one of them...

That's what you're here for;

You'll destroy me in the end.

Lesson for Life

When you're broken inside

And you look at the world

Through hazy eyes,

From the shattered

Pieces of glass

A new window may emerge,

And through it you'll see me

When you need me,

And I'll be there

Whenever you need any help.

But will I ever see you?

Will you ever come to me

On the days I'm unable to move?

Or will you even take away my privilege

Of being able to comfort you,

If I treat you too nicely?

Did I lose all my value

The moment I stopped being a fantasy?

Is it my lesson for life

That I shall be punished

For opening my heart

And daring to love?

Is this sacred knowledge

The only gift you'll ever give me?

My Beautiful Words

Is that it?

Crickets...

Is there really nothing on your mind?

I just poured my heart out,

Careful not to use that one special word,

Which I'm withholding for now,

Hoping I can utter it in the future,

At a more suitable time,

Preferably to you,

And preferably you'd want to hear it, too.

It's not time for that yet.

I just wanted to give you a preview

Of my heart's content.

Does it not mean anything to you?

Do you not care?

Do you rather spend your waking moments

Hating the orange man

Than loving a lady in black,

With lips of passionate red,

Who wants nothing but a little loving back?

I'd love to say, 'it's your loss'...

That's what I'm told to think.

But you really don't know

What you could possible use,

While I know exactly how happy

Just one loving word from you

Would make me.

And you finally answer...

You thank me for my beautiful words

And tell me that you're honoured

That I've shared my feelings with you.

That was it...

Slow, lukewarm, obligatory.

Yet I'm still hoping...

You then say I can tell you anything.

'You're safe with me,' you reassure me.

But am I really as safe as you suggest?

Do you think you can protect me from myself?

I hope my beautiful words make you feel good.

Can you at least please treasure them?

There's no one I'd have rather given them to,

And I have none left to give anyone else.

Ouroboros

The snake bites its own tail

And loses and finds itself

In a twisted dance

Poisoning its own body

Devouring greedily

What's still left

With eyes fixed on infinity

It yearns for its own end

The hungry ego

Under the spell

Of the primeval libido

And the divine mortido

It knows it cannot win

The fuller it grows

The more it loses

The flesh yearns for meat

Focused on the most primal of urges

To feed

And to be consumed

By something it once feared

When anticipation replaces gloom

In my dream

The snake was slowly eating itself

But it looked so serene

There was no blood

No signs of agony

No moments of doubt

There's no room for hesitation

When you can't feel cold anymore

The purest love radiates from your destination

And there's no fear, only the naked soul

Swimming in a blissful light

Until in bliss you finally drown

And the snake gets distracted

It looks at me

And lets go of its tail

The world disintegrates

There's nowhere to escape

But the bite causes no pain

The poison rushes through the elated heart

It's so warm in the embrace of the snake

Just ask Cleopatra

While Anubis awaits

Printed in Great Britain
by Amazon